D0899974

CROCODILES

VING WILD

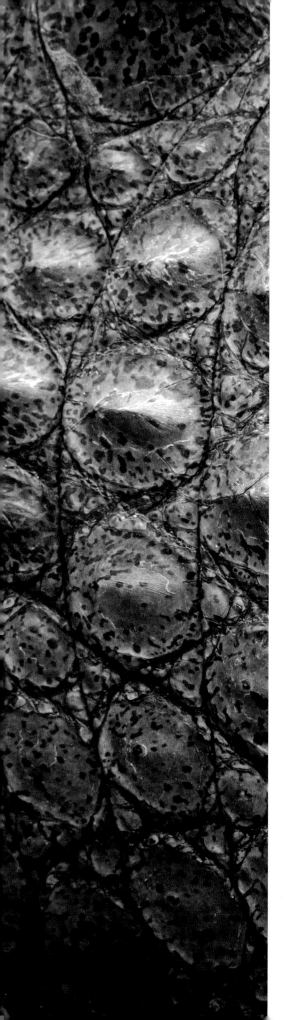

# LIVING WILD

Published by Creative Education
P.O. Box 227, Mankato, Minnesota 56002
Creative Education is an imprint of The Creative Company
www.thecreativecompany.us

Design and production by Mary Herrmann
Art direction by Rita Marshall
Printed in the United States of America

Photographs by 123RF (Oleksandr Onyshchenko, Whitekrechet), Alamy (JONATHAN AYRES), Corbis (Yann Arthus-Bertrand, Jonathan Blair), Dreamstime (Goborut, Jonaldm, Johnandersonphoto, Koshar, Michaf, Ncbateman1, Pdiaz, Photomyeye, Photosbyash, Robyvannucci, Siloto, Sumos), Getty Images (Annie Griffiths Belt, Randy Olson, Joe Raedle, JEFFREY L. ROTMAN, Justin Sullivan), iStockphoto (John Anderson, Paul Benefield, Michael Buckley, Franck Camhi, Hirlesteanu Dumitru, Olivia Falvey, Erik Gauger, Jonathan Heger, Keiichi Hiki, Liz Leyden, Daryl Marquardt, Lee Pettet, Mike Rogal, Nicola Stratford, Mark Weiss), Minden Pictures (Suzi Eszterhas, Mike Parry)

Library of Congress Cataloging-in-Publication Data
Gish, Melissa.
Crocodiles / by Melissa Gish.
p. cm. — (Living wild)
Includes bibliographical references and index.
ISBN 978-1-58341-738-6
1. Crocodiles—Juvenile literature. I. Title. II. Series.

QL666.C925G57 2009
597.98'2—dc22      2008009501

First Edition
9 8 7 6 5 4 3 2 1

**CREATIVE EDUCATION**

# CROCODILES

Melissa Gish

The swamp is calm. Frogs hum quietly
in the tall grass, while long-necked birds

peck at the ground. A soft splash
signals that a crocodile has surfaced.

The swamp is calm. Frogs hum quietly in the tall grass, while long-necked birds peck at the ground. A soft splash signals that a crocodile has surfaced. It is a male; he hears a muffled sound from underground that beckons him to shore. The crocodile joins his mate at their nest in the sand. The female begins digging up the nest, uncovering 30 eggs that quiver in the warm, moist earth. She and the male lift the eggs out of the nest and begin gently rolling them inside their mouths. The eggshells start to crack. As the eggs fall back into the nest, tiny baby crocodiles emerge, breaking free of their shells. They are immediately ready to swim. The crocodile parents scoop the babies up in their mouths and carry them into the water. After swimming with their parents for a month, the young crocodiles will make their own ways in the world.

# WHERE IN THE WORLD THEY LIVE

 **Nile Crocodile** along the Nile delta and Red Sea; parts of western, central, and southern Africa; western Madagascar

 **American Crocodile** southern tip of Florida; Costa Rica; from Mexico through northern South America

 **Saltwater Crocodile** throughout Southeast Asia, northern Australia, and surrounding waters

 **Slender-snouted Crocodile** western and central Africa

**Siamese Crocodile** Indonesia, Thailand, Vietnam, Myanmar, East Malaysia, Brunei, Laos, and Cambodia

 **Dwarf Crocodile** western and central Africa

**Orinoco Crocodile** (not pictured) northern South America near Orinoco River

The 13 species of crocodile are found in tropical or desert-like regions on five of Earth's continents. With the exception of the saltwater crocodile, which sometimes travels far out to sea, most species dwell in lakes, rivers, and marshes. The colored squares represent the common locations of each species.

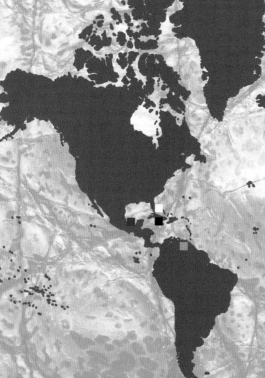

 **Philippine Crocodile** the Philippines

 **Cuban Crocodile** Cuba's Zapata Swamp and Isle of Youth

 **Freshwater Crocodile** northern Australia

 **Morelet's Crocodile or Mexican Crocodile** parts of Central America along the Gulf of Mexico

 **New Guinea Crocodile** island of New Guinea

 **Indian Crocodile** throughout the Indian subcontinent

## LIVING FOSSILS

The crocodile is considered to be a living fossil. This amazing creature has survived virtually unchanged since the days of the dinosaurs. The 13 species of crocodile living today are found on five of Earth's seven continents: North and South America, Asia, Africa, and Australia. They belong to the family Crocodylidae. The name "crocodile" comes from the Greek words *kroke*, which means "pebbles," and *drilos*, which means "worm." The name was given to the animals by Greek writers who saw them basking on the stony shores of Egypt's Nile River. Considered holy animals, crocodiles were respected by the ancient Egyptians, who had 20 different names for them.

Crocodiles are reptiles. Reptiles are ectothermic animals, meaning that their body temperatures change with the environment. When a crocodile's body temperature gets too low, it must warm itself in the sun. When its body temperature gets too high, it must cool itself in shade, mud, or water. While most reptiles move slowly to conserve energy and body warmth, an attacking crocodile can move swiftly, both on land

**Depending on the species, a crocodile can have 60 to 86 teeth, all of which fall out and are replaced 2 to 3 times a year.**

and in the water. Most reptiles, including crocodiles, reproduce by laying eggs.

The earliest crocodile ancestors appeared about 200 million years ago. These ancient crocodiles were 10 to 40 feet (3–12 m) long. Millions of years later, when most of the large reptiles died out, crocodiles and their closest relatives—birds—survived. As they **evolved**, these *crocodilians* moved from dry land to murky swamps and slow-moving rivers, changing into the crocodiles we know today.

Crocodiles are related to other reptiles such as caimans and gharials, but the reptiles they are most often confused with are alligators. The main difference between the two is easy to spot up-close. When an alligator's mouth is closed, its teeth are hidden. But a crocodile's teeth are always visible in an interlocking pattern, and it has an enormous fourth tooth on the lower jaw that juts up behind its nostrils. Also, while an alligator has a wide, U-shaped snout, a crocodile has a long, narrow, V-shaped snout.

The dwarf crocodile is the smallest species of crocodile, averaging five feet (1.5 m) in length. Australia's

A crocodile spends much of its time basking in the sun to keep its body temperature regulated and warm.

*Crocodiles do not normally stay underwater for longer than 15 minutes at a time, even though they can survive longer.*

saltwater crocodile can grow to be 23 feet (7 m) in length and weigh up to 2,200 pounds (998 kg), making it the largest reptile on Earth. No matter the species, all crocodiles' bodies are covered with scales—thick ones on the upper body and slightly thinner ones on the underside of the body. Every scale has a tiny pit, called a **dermal** pressure receptor, which helps the crocodile detect such things as changes in water pressure, movement of prey in the water, and water **salinity**.

The crocodile can move swiftly on land, and **webbed** hind feet that can be tucked close to the body make it a powerfully streamlined swimmer. Crocodiles have five toes on each front foot and four on each back foot. The inner three toes on each foot have powerful claws, and the remaining toes are stumpy. Crocodiles use their claws to hold prey to the ground or underwater. Crocodiles walk on the bottom of rivers and swamps, and their sharp claws help them move along muddy surfaces. Female crocodiles use their claws to dig holes into which they can lay their eggs.

Like a living submarine, a crocodile can float or sink at will. It can expand its lungs, adjusting its ability to float, and can stay completely underwater for up to three hours. As it goes underwater, a crocodile's ears and nostrils automatically close tightly. A nictitating (*NIK-tih-tayt-ing*) membrane (a see-through inner eyelid) lowers over its eyes. When it catches its prey, the entire tongue, which is

*The thick skin of a crocodile's legs is firm but flexible, allowing the crocodile to stretch and run.*

**Crocodiles are swift on land; the Nile crocodile has been known to dash at speeds of up to 30 miles (48 km) per hour.**

By tipping their heads back, crocodiles can judge the distance to overhead prey with great accuracy.

attached to the bottom of the mouth, works like a stopper to plug the crocodile's throat. A bony pouch in the throat called the gular blocks the airway but allows the crocodile to eat while submerged.

Crocodiles eat meat and will feed on almost anything they can catch—mammals that drink at the water's edge, birds, fish, and even humans. Most deadly encounters with crocodiles occur in Africa, Asia, and Australia, where humans share crocodile habitats. Crocodiles are cannibalistic, meaning they will eat their own kind. Adult crocodiles commonly feed on younger, smaller crocodiles. They will kill crocodile hatchlings as well as old or injured crocodiles that cannot defend themselves.

The swamps of southern Florida, the only place in North America where crocodiles live, are home to the American crocodile. Other crocodiles around the world live in a variety of environments, from freshwater rivers and swamps to **brackish** wetlands. Some even live by the ocean. All crocodiles hunt by ambushing their prey. Whether in the water, with only their eyes and nostrils visible, or on land, **camouflaged** on a muddy shore or in tall grass, a crocodile will stay motionless for long periods of time, waiting for prey to come close enough to be grabbed with a sudden strike.

Crocodiles have the strongest bite of any animal on Earth. Even a great white shark's bite, at 400 pounds of pressure per square inch (281,228 kg/sq m), or psi, is no match for a crocodile's bite of 5,000 psi (3.5 million kg/ sq m). In contrast, a human's strongest bite is only about 200 psi (140,614 kg/sq m). Once a crocodile shuts its mouth, it is nearly impossible to pry it open. Despite having such powerful jaws, a crocodile never chews its food. Rather, it tilts its head upward and lets the food drop down its throat.

If water becomes too scarce, crocodiles will migrate long distances in search of better habitats. Saltwater crocodiles will travel as far as 560 miles (901 km) up and down Australia's coast. They sometimes even swim up to 18 miles (29 km) out to sea, where they rest in coral caves on the Great Barrier Reef. Crocodiles seem to have a homing instinct, as they will return to their old territories when water levels change in new habitats. Some crocodiles have even been known to travel as far as 250 miles (402 km) to return home after being relocated by scientists.

Crocodile eggs look very similar in size and shape to the eggs laid by geese, but crocodile eggs have a much thinner shell.

Even when large groups of crocodiles are gathered together in one small place, they rarely fight over food.

## DEADLY STATUES

O n a typical day, a crocodile may look more like a statue than a living creature. Crocodiles are inactive most of the time. They have a very slow **metabolism** and can go long periods of time without any food—up to a year for large adults. In order to **thermoregulate** their bodies, crocodiles spend their days basking in the sun, soaking in the water, or hiding in a burrow—all the time waiting for prey to come close enough to grab.

A group of crocodiles is named for its activity. On land, a group is called a "bask," and in the water, it is called a "float." As crocodiles bask in the sun, they hold their mouths open. This is known as gaping and may be done for a variety of reasons. Gaping allows the crocodile to save time when attacking prey. Also, while gaping, a crocodile will allow certain birds to pick its teeth and clean up bits of food, fungus, and **parasites** from its mouth. Crocodiles also gape when it rains, and they gape at night. This behavior has led scientists to consider that gaping may also be a social behavior, though they are not sure what messages crocodiles may be communicating by doing it.

*Crocodiles will camouflage themselves to hide from prey and adapt quickly to avoid dangerous situations.*

Most crocodile species gather in large groups controlled by a dominant male who is highly territorial. Despite living in communities, most crocodile species do not hunt in groups. An exception is the Nile crocodile, which is much more social than other species such as the saltwater crocodile. As herds of such animals as zebras and wildebeest migrate across rivers, teams of Nile crocodiles surround the animals, cut off escape routes, and lunge at their prey from all angles. Depending on the size of the prey, Nile crocodiles will sometimes even share their meals with one another.

Crocodiles kill land prey by drowning the animal. No meal is too small, and no scraps are left behind. A crocodile will eat an animal's entire body—including the fur, feathers, hooves, and bones. It will also eat stones, which help grind up the food in the crocodile's stomach, to aid in digestion. It takes about 72 hours for a crocodile's meal to be fully digested and excreted as waste. Cool temperatures may further slow the rate of digestion.

To protect themselves from bad weather, crocodiles use their snouts and feet to dig burrows. The entrance to a burrow may be just below the surface of a riverbank or

Once it has a firm grip on prey such as a wildebeest, a crocodile will not let go until it has drowned it.

even underwater and may extend from 10 to 30 feet (3–9 m) inland. The narrow burrow is wide enough for only one crocodile to turn around inside it. Crocodiles prefer privacy and do not share their burrows—not even with their mates.

Crocodile mating occurs once a year. Males make a show of attracting females. They slap the water with their snouts, blow water noisily from their nostrils,

*Crocodile mating occurs in the dry season, when water levels are down and sandy shores for nesting (opposite) are more abundant.*

grunt, bellow, and groan. A female is very selective when choosing a partner and may reject many males before allowing one to get close to her. Larger, healthier males are usually the ones who win a mate. A compatible pair of crocodiles will rub their jaws together and make croaking noises before retreating to the water to mate.

About two months after mating, the female makes a nest in which to lay her eggs. Because crocodiles need air to survive, even as they develop inside an egg, mothers must lay their eggs on land that is high enough to be above the danger of flooding. A crocodile inside an egg cannot survive underwater for more than 12 hours. Also, crocodile eggs will not develop unless their temperature remains between 80 and 94 °F (27 to 34 °C). Instinct tells the crocodile where to make its nest, and it uses the same place year after year.

The mother crocodile uses her snout and feet to build a nest out of sand, mud, and weeds. It looks like a shallow hole. Depending on the species, the crocodile then lays between 20 and 90 eggs. Temperature determines the gender of the developing eggs. Males develop at around 89 °F (32 °C), and females develop at lower or higher

If crocodile hatchlings are in danger, the mother may scoop them up and flip them into her mouth or throat pouch for protection.

temperatures. The mother will watch over her nest for 90 days. The father also shares in the duty of guarding the nest from predators such as birds, snakes, lizards, and other crocodiles.

When they are ready to hatch, the baby crocodiles will make a chirping sound. The mother then digs up the eggs. The hatchlings aren't very strong at first. They may have trouble escaping the egg, despite being born with an **egg tooth**. A parent may help its offspring emerge by gently cracking the shell in its mouth to speed up the process.

Hatchlings are about eight inches (20 cm) long at birth. They are green or gray with black stripes. This coloring helps them hide from hungry predators. The hatchlings are ready to swim and begin feeding immediately. If the nest is near a water source, the mother crocodile will simply direct her young to the water. If the nest is farther from the water, the mother may scoop up the babies in her mouth and carry them to the river or lake. They will remain close to their mother for a month or two. Only two percent of offspring will make it to adulthood, the rest falling victim to disease or predators.

The crocodile is an apex predator, which means that it stands at the top of the **food chain**. Because an adult crocodile's only threat is from humans, it may live up to 70 years in the wild if left undisturbed. Even though the crocodile was once respected and even revered as a god in some cultures, today it is considered a pest by many people. Viewed as an inconvenient and dangerous predator, the crocodile has been hunted to near extinction around the world. In fact, in the land where it was once most loved—northern Egypt—the Nile crocodile is rarely seen.

*Between 80 and 90 percent of crocodile eggs that are laid hatch, but the survival rate for hatchlings is low.*

In Egyptian artwork and architecture, the god Sobek was represented as having a human body and a crocodile's head.

## SPIRIT OF THE CROCODILE

*Nile crocodiles' brains and hearts are the most advanced among reptiles, their four-chambered hearts most resembling those of birds.*

Egypt's Nile River valley, the birthplace of one of the world's oldest civilizations, is among the most fascinating and mysterious places in history. Crocodiles have played a major role in this history. Sobek was an ancient Egyptian god of crocodiles. More than 3,000 years ago, his devotees believed that he created the Nile River. The powerful crocodile then became a symbol of the Egyptian pharoahs, or kings, and many crocodile statues were made in their honor.

The Egyptian people believed that Sobek laid the world's first eggs, which gave life to plants, animals, and people. Temples were built to honor crocodiles, and some crocodiles were even **mummified** like important people. The crocodile of ancient Egypt was largely respected and feared by people. In some places, crocodiles were kept as pets in fenced-in ponds or elaborate stone pools. In more remote areas, where people knew little of the pharoahs' religious rituals, people killed crocodiles out of mistrust or to keep them from invading farmland near the river.

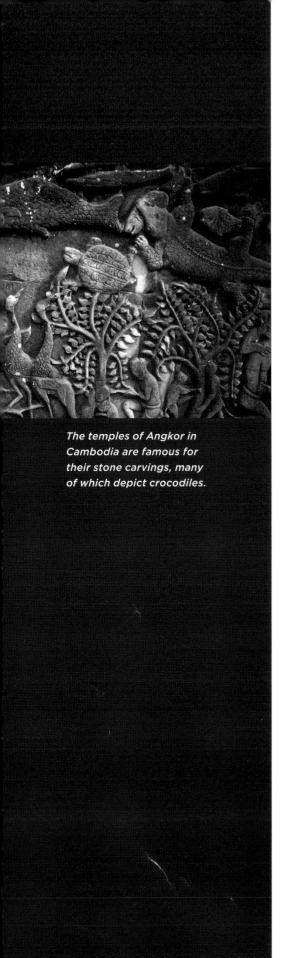

The temples of Angkor in Cambodia are famous for their stone carvings, many of which depict crocodiles.

On the island of Madagascar, off the eastern coast of Africa, some people still consider crocodiles to be sacred and believe that crocodiles are the **reincarnated** spirits of their ancestors. In Guinea, a nation on Africa's western coast, crocodiles are respected for being important parts of the environment and local culture. The people hold ceremonies that include the wearing of masks depicting the crocodile.

On the world's second-largest island, New Guinea, the Iatmul people have worshiped the crocodile for generations. The Yenchenmangua Village is home to a crocodile **cult**. The people there believe a giant crocodile created the world. According to their ancient tradition, when boys are about 13 years old, they have their tribe's markings carved into their skin. The boys are then sent into the jungle to survive on their own for many weeks. After the boys have endured this hardship and pain, the cuts heal into raised scars that resemble scaly crocodile skin. The boys are then said to be filled with the "crocodile spirit."

In Karachi, Pakistan, a group of people known as the Siddi built a shrine to an ancient holy person named Pir Mangho. Crocodiles, which are thought to be the messengers of Pir Mangho, live in a lake near the shrine. This area is also filled with hot springs. Pir Mangho's followers believe that the hot springs and the crocodiles

Crocodiles have made their way into modern architecture in places such as Australia's Gagudju Crocodile Holiday Inn.

were gifts from Pir Mangho's angels. The scientific explanation for the crocodiles' presence is that the reptiles were carried to the region in a heavy flood thousands of years ago and settled in the lake. Pir Mangho's followers hold a week-long festival at the shrine each year to celebrate the crocodiles. People come from far away to make wishes by throwing fresh meat to the crocodiles. The festival ends with a ceremony in which flowers are draped around the neck of the oldest, biggest crocodile, called the chief crocodile. He is called Mor Sahib, after a beloved spirit.

The tradition of crocodile worship may be long-standing, but a new set of beliefs has emerged more recently. In Tainan, Taiwan, a temple is home to a dead

crocodile, which was stuffed and brought there in the 1980s. Some people in the city believe that by visiting the temple and touching the crocodile's back, they will be cured of sickness and that evil spirits will flee from them. Live, captive crocodiles on a farm near the temple are also visited; there, people pray for good luck and health.

Crocodiles are popularly portrayed as villains in stories and movies. Sometimes they are comical, as in British author J. M. Barrie's 1911 book *Peter and Wendy*, which was made into the Disney movie *Peter Pan* in 1953. In the story, a grumpy, grinning crocodile bites off Captain Hook's hand and eventually eats him. In the 1977 Disney movie *The Rescuers*, a pair of crocodiles serve the criminal

*Crocodiles have a complex social structure that uses a ranking system and assigns dominance to a large male.*

Moving in an S-shaped pattern of zigzags, most crocodiles can swim up to 20 miles (32 km) per hour.

Madame Medusa, and in *The Emperor's New Groove* (2000), a crocodile is kept in a pit to serve the Emperor's scheming adviser Yzma. The American comic strip *Pearls Before Swine*, created by Stephan Pastis in 2001, features the antics of the Fraternity of Crocodiles (also known as "Zeeba Zeeba Eata"), a dim-witted group that repeatedly fails at hunting.

However, crocodiles are sometimes depicted as smart and even friendly. In the 2006 Disney movie *The Wild*, a pair of crocodiles—pets who had been flushed into the sewer—look tough and scary. But they turn out to be friendly fellows who guide the lion Samson and his zoo-animal friends to the harbor rather than eat them. On American television, the show *Christopher Crocodile* features a playful crocodile who leaves his native "Mudagascar" to help the people of "Muddytown" by inventing wonderful gadgets such as a flying bicycle to blow away the clouds.

Sometimes crocodiles are portrayed as dangerous monsters. In British author Roald Dahl's 1978 book *The Enormous Crocodile*, a mean-spirited reptile wants to eat children despite being told by other animals that eating

# HOW DOTH THE LITTLE CROCODILE

How doth the little crocodile
Improve his shining tail,
And pour the waters of the Nile
On every golden scale!

How cheerfully he seems to grin,
How neatly spreads his claws,
And welcomes little fishes in,
With gently smiling jaws!

*Lewis Carroll (1832–1898)*
*from* Alice's Adventures in Wonderland

*Steve Irwin, "The Crocodile Hunter," had a soft spot for alligators as well as crocodiles and other reptiles.*

children is wrong. And in the comic-book world of *Batman*, crocodiles live beneath Gotham City and are ruled by the Sewer King, who uses them to keep people away from his lair and to perform criminal deeds such as stealing and kidnapping.

Real crocodiles cannot be trained to obey commands, but they can appear to smile for the camera. One person who helped popularize crocodiles on television was Steve Irwin, who was also known as "The Crocodile Hunter." Irwin became world-famous from his television shows, wildlife documentaries, and the 2002 movie *Crocodile Hunter: Collision Course.* He hosted many shows with his wife, Terri, from their home at the Australia Zoo in Queensland, Australia, which was founded by his parents. Irwin traveled all over the world to film wildlife, and he is probably best known for bringing the plight of the endangered saltwater crocodile to the public's attention. He died in 2006, but in his lifetime, Irwin founded two conservation groups, Wildlife Warriors Worldwide and International Crocodile Rescue, both of which continue his legacy of caring for the Earth's animals—especially crocodiles.

A six-foot (1.8 m) saltwater crocodile with its jaws taped shut chases swimmers at an Australian swimming club, helping them increase their speed.

The best territories—with the best hunting opportunities—are guarded ferociously by the strongest males.

## STILL STRUGGLING

As cities grow and more people move into crocodile habitats, the number of conflicts between humans and crocodiles increases. Hundreds of people suffer attacks each year, but crocodiles are also victims. Fear and lack of education about crocodiles has led to their widespread slaughter. Scientists are now working to try to reverse this trend and make crocodiles and humans safe from one another.

The first crocodiles appeared about 200 million years ago. The earliest crocodile fossils have been found in Australia and India, but prehistoric crocodiles inhabited all areas of the Southern Hemisphere. Wherever there were rivers or swamps, there were usually crocodiles.

Early humans gathered crocodile eggs and sometimes hunted crocodiles for food. Up until the mid-1800s, crocodiles were abundant in all of their original habitats. But as Europeans began to **colonize** Africa and India, they put a high value on the many natural resources found in those countries, including ivory from elephants, fur from monkeys, and the uniquely textured skin of crocodiles. Millions of crocodiles were killed, and their hides were

**In 2001, a 16-inch (41 cm) crocodile was fished out of Austria's Danube River—nowhere near its natural habitat and never claimed as a pet.**

Crocodile belts can cost about $500, while boots can sell for $3,000 a pair.

The interlocking scales on a crocodile's hide are called scutes. The bony plates that offer armorlike protection are called osteoderms.

shipped back to Europe to be sold. Crocodile populations fell drastically. American crocodiles in Florida, saltwater crocodiles in Australia, and many crocodile species in South America all suffered similar fates. By the time worldwide conservation efforts began to focus on crocodiles in the 1970s, hunters had nearly wiped out these reptiles.

Education is the main goal of most crocodile research projects around the world. Scientists want to learn more about crocodiles in order to save them from becoming the victims of fear and mistrust. Research has determined that crocodiles are able to survive in developed areas as long as they are not being deliberately killed. To aid scientific efforts to study crocodiles in the wild, many countries have now put laws in place to protect crocodiles. However, few countries have the resources to enforce these laws, and **poaching** often goes unpunished. Crocodile hides bring sellers $200 million a year.

Captive-breeding is a potential solution to the high demand for crocodile hides and meat. **Captive-reared** crocodiles provide skins for leather products and meat for food, thus eliminating the need for hunting wild crocodiles. In addition, some tourists pay to be able to

shoot a crocodile, and providing such opportunities through crocodile ranches means that more money will go toward rearing more captive crocodiles. This practice is proving particularly successful in South Africa, where Nile crocodiles are ranch-raised.

Captive-breeding is also used to reintroduce depleted populations of crocodiles into the wild. When a program to rebuild the saltwater crocodile population in Northern Territory, Australia, began in 1972, fewer than 5,000 of these animals lived in the territory's coastal swamps. The government plan had landowners collect crocodile eggs and

*Crocodiles are smart, planning their hunting behavior to match the activity of their intended prey.*

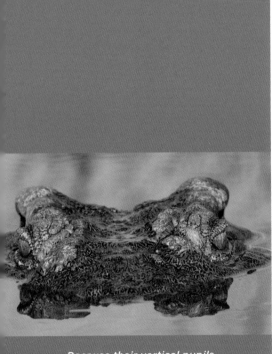

*Because their vertical pupils can open wide to let in light, crocodiles have good vision, even at night.*

sell them to researchers rather than destroy them as they had been doing. By making live crocodiles more valuable than dead ones, the program succeeded in saving the species, as researchers then allowed the eggs to hatch and released the young. The plan has increased the population of saltwater crocodiles in Northern Territory to about 70,000.

While the Northern Territory project involves rearing saltwater crocodiles outside their natural habitats, such research and conservation groups as the Crocodile Rehabilitation, Observance and Conservation Project (CROC) are involved in what is called in-situ research. This means that the animals are studied in their original environments. Observers stake out areas of habitat where crocodiles live, and then they simply watch the animals' behaviors. The crocodiles' movements, feeding habits, and nesting behaviors are recorded. This information will help people avoid deadly encounters with crocodiles by knowing when crocodiles might show more aggression, such as while they are mating or protecting their hatchlings.

The Wildlife Conservation Society is working with wildlife protection agencies and local communities in seven countries of Southeast Asia to improve crocodile conservation. Scientists first count the crocodiles and measure their available habitat. Then they create management plans—suggesting additional protected areas, captive-breeding programs, and the relocation of wild crocodiles—to improve the animal's numbers.

Other types of research are conducted to better understand how crocodiles swim, eat, and communicate. For example, studies have shown that crocodiles are the most vocal of all reptiles. Zoologist Adam Britton is well known for his research on crocodile sounds. He has recorded and studied what he calls "Croc Talk" for many years. Crocodiles are known to make more than 20 different sounds—from chirps and hisses to grunts and growls—and each sound has a distinct meaning, such as "I feel threatened" or "I want your meal." Some messages are sent underwater. The crocodile will vibrate its throat muscles, sending sounds that travel four times faster and farther than they would travel on land. Some sounds are even made at **frequencies** too low to be heard by human ears.

The Crocodile Specialist Group (CSG) has determined that habitat loss is the second-biggest threat to crocodiles.

**Crocodillin is an antibacterial substance in crocodiles' blood that protects them from infections caused by dirty water.**

*When scientists have easy access to crocodiles, they are better able to study the animal's characteristics and behavior.*

A recent study focused on Central and South America. In such countries as Argentina, Bolivia, and Paraguay, wetlands are being made into farmland and urban areas. In Brazil, particularly, wetlands are lost when dams are built to provide hydroelectric power. And pollution caused by industries located along rivers has a negative effect on what remains of the crocodiles' habitat.

In North America, crocodiles are found only in southern Florida, and today, people tend to leave them alone. In 1976, a pair of American crocodiles was spotted at the Turkey Point Nuclear Generating Station, which is located near Biscayne National Park,

south of Miami. Scientists immediately began studying the crocodiles, which had recently been placed on the endangered species list. Now, more than 30 years later, a body of continuously recycled water at this power plant is home to more than 80 crocodiles, which are protected by law.

As one of nature's top predators, crocodiles are vital to the health of food chains around the world. Yet researchers have only begun to learn the mysteries of their long history on the planet. There is no doubt that these amazing reptiles have more secrets to share, if only they can survive long enough to reveal them.

## ANIMAL TALE: THE STORY OF TIMOR

**The island of Timor, located about 400 miles (643 km) north of Australia, is home to the saltwater crocodile. The people of Timor regard this ancient creature as a proud and strong spirit who helped create their homeland. The following story explains how the island was formed and why the people respect the crocodile.**

Many years ago in a faraway place, a little crocodile lived among many large relatives in a big swamp. The larger crocodiles often chased the little crocodile away from prey or snatched food right out of his jaws. He felt very sad, and as he watched his relatives bask on the shore or cruise in the swamp, he dreamed of becoming a big crocodile like them. Days and nights passed, and soon the little crocodile weakened from hunger. As he looked around at the swamp,

he grew sadder and lonelier. And he felt that the swamp wasn't really home for him.

One day, the little crocodile decided to leave the swamp. He headed across the land to the open sea to find food and chase his dream of becoming a big crocodile. Before long, however, the day grew too hot for the little crocodile, and he was still far from the seashore. Rapidly drying out and feeling exhausted, the little crocodile collapsed and prepared to die under the rays of the baking sun.

A small boy who was walking home from gathering fruit saw the stranded crocodile lying in the sun and took pity on him. He picked up the little crocodile and carried him to the sea. The crocodile instantly revived in the refreshing water and felt very grateful.

"Little boy," he said, "you saved my life. If I can repay

you someday, please call on me. I will be at your command." With that, the little crocodile swam away across the sea.

Several years later, the boy, who was now a strong man, went to the edge of the sea and called out to the crocodile. "Brother Crocodile!" he called, "I, too, have a dream! I want to see the world! Come back to repay your debt to me!"

The little crocodile, who was not little anymore but was also big and strong, came to the boy. "Climb on my back," said the crocodile, "and tell me where you want to go."

"Follow the sun," said the boy.

The crocodile set off for the east. He and the boy traveled the oceans for many years. They saw many wonderful sights, and their friendship grew. The crocodile was no longer lonely. Wherever he and the boy went, he felt like it was home.

One day he said to the man, "Brother, we have been traveling for a long time, and I am grateful for your friendship. But I am old, and the time has come for me to die. In memory of your kindness, I will turn myself into a beautiful island where you and your children can live until the sun sinks into the sea."

As the crocodile died, he grew bigger, and taller, and stronger. His ridged back became great mountains. His scales became rolling hills. He transformed himself into the island of Timor.

Now, when the people of Timor swim in the ocean, they enter the water saying, "Don't eat me crocodile, I am your family."

## GLOSSARY

**antibacterial** – active against bacteria, or living organisms that cannot be seen except under a microscope

**brackish** – containing a mixture of salt water and fresh water

**camouflaged** – hidden, due to coloring or markings that blend in with a given environment

**captive-reared** – raised in a place from which escape is not possible

**colonize** – to establish settlements in a new land and exercise control over them

**cult** – a group of people who share the same beliefs or ideals

**dermal** – of or relating to the skin, which is also called dermis

**egg tooth** – a hard, toothlike tip of a young bird's beak or a young reptile's mouth, used only for breaking through its egg

**evolved** – gradually developed into a new form

**food chain** – a system in nature in which living things are dependent on each other for food

**frequencies** – the measurements of sound waves

**metabolism** – the processes that keep a body alive, including making use of food for energy

**mummified** – when a body has been preserved from decay by being filled and covered with herbs, oils, and cloth

**parasites** – animals or plants that live on or inside another living thing (called a host) while giving nothing back to the host; some parasites cause disease or even death

**poaching** – hunting or stealing protected species of animals, even though doing so is against the law

**regurgitate** – to throw up partially digested food

**reincarnated** – born again in a new body or form

**salinity** – the amount of salt in water

**thermoregulate** – to keep the body's internal temperature within certain boundaries regardless of the environmental temperature

**webbed** – connected by a web (of skin, as in the case of webbed feet)

## SELECTED BIBLIOGRAPHY

Alderton, David. *Crocodiles and Alligators of the World.* New York: Facts on File, 2004.

Crocodile Specialist Group. "Homepage." Florida Museum of Natural History. http://www.flmnh.ufl.edu/herpetology/Crocs.htm.

Garnett, Stephen. *Crocodiles and Alligators.* New York: Checkmark Books, 1989.

International Crocodile Rescue. "Homepage." Australia Zoo. http://www.internationalcrocodilerescue.com.au/about_rescue_unit/index.html.

Kelly, Lynne. *Crocodile: Evolution's Greatest Survivor.* St. Leonards, New South Wales, Australia: Allen & Unwin, 2007.

Murphy, James B., and Neil Schlager. *Grzimek's Animal Life Encyclopedia*, 2nd ed. Vol. 7, *Reptiles*. New York: Gale Group, 2003.

Crocodiles may use their powerful tails to launch their bodies vertically out of the water to grab prey.

# INDEX